I0814822

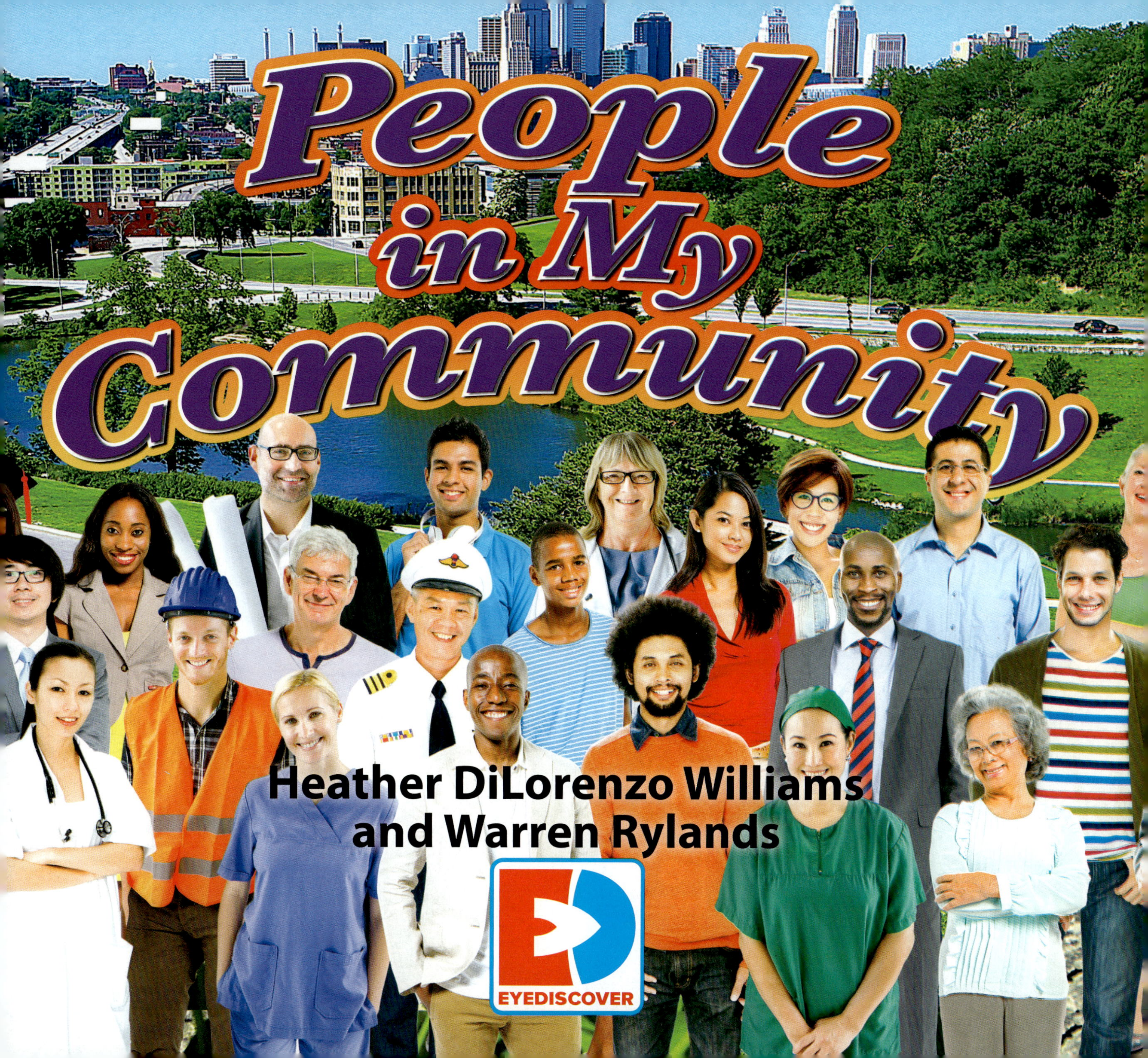
People in My Community
Heather DiLorenzo Williams
and Warren Rylands
EYEDISCOVER

Go to **www.eyediscover.com** and enter this book's unique code.

BOOK CODE

AVY84389

EYEDISCOVER brings you optic readalongs that support active learning.

Published by AV² by Weigl
350 5th Avenue, 59th Floor New York, NY 10118
Website: www.eyediscover.com

Library of Congress Control Number: 2018953520

ISBN 978-1-4896-8051-8 (hardcover)

Printed in Brainerd, Minnesota,United States
1 2 3 4 5 6 7 8 9 0 22 21 20 19 18

082018
120917

Project Coordinators: John Willis
Designer: Mandy Christiansen

Weigl acknowledges Getty Images, Alamy, iStock, and Shutterstock as the primary image suppliers for this title.

EYEDISCOVER provides enriched content, optimized for tablet use, that supplements and complements this book. EYEDISCOVER books strive to create inspired learning and engage young minds in a total learning experience.

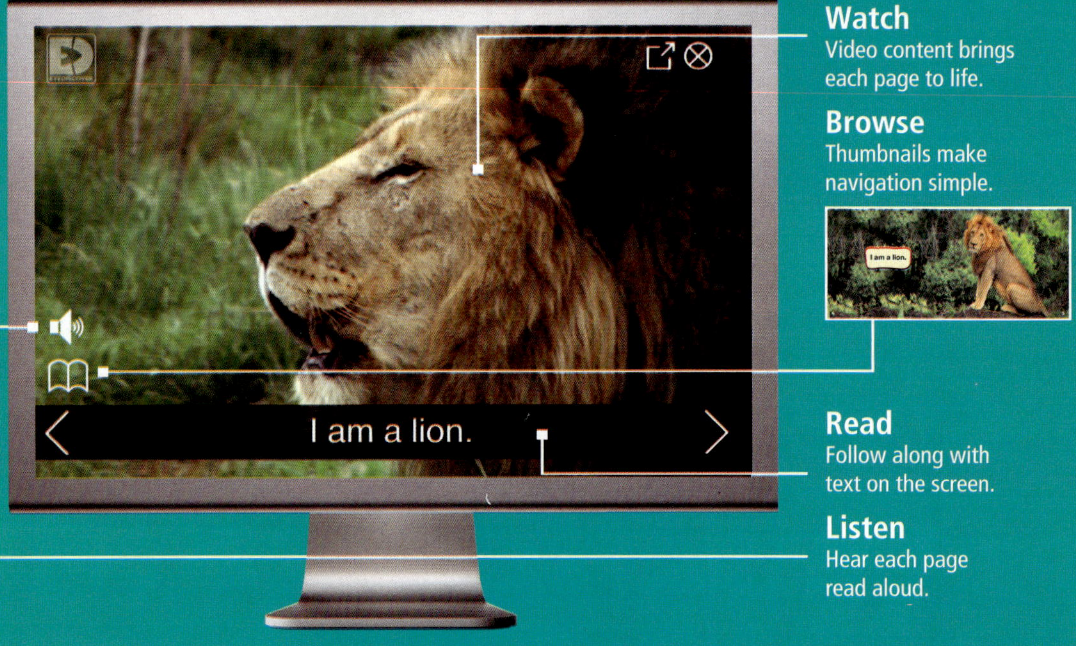

Watch
Video content brings each page to life.

Browse
Thumbnails make navigation simple.

Read
Follow along with text on the screen.

Listen
Hear each page read aloud.

Your EYEDISCOVER Optic Readalongs come alive with...

Audio
Listen to the entire book read aloud.

Video
High resolution videos turn each spread into an optic readalong.

OPTIMIZED FOR

AND MUCH MORE!

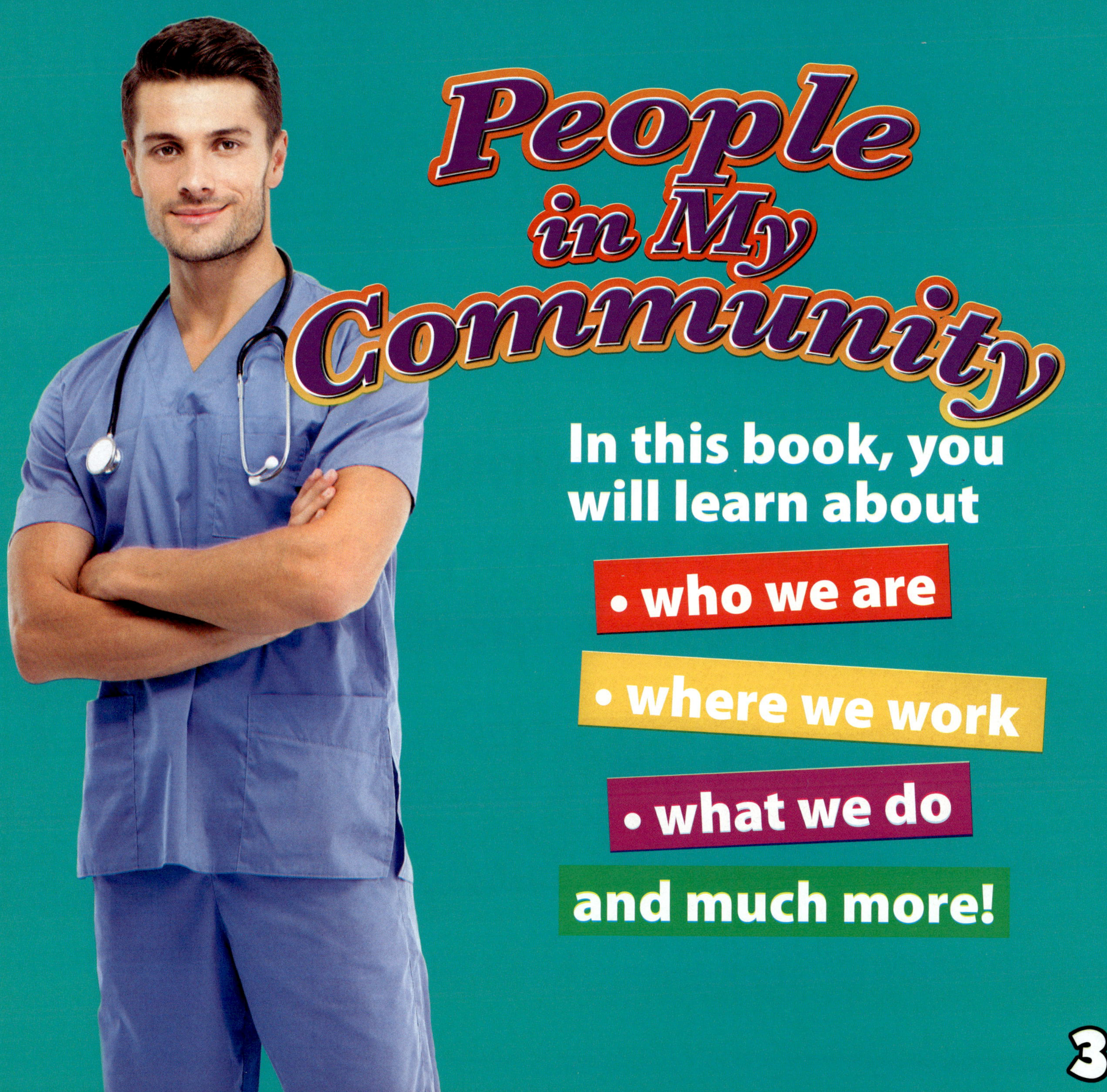
People in My Community
In this book, you will learn about
• who we are
• where we work
• what we do
and much more!

A community is a place where people live, work, and play.

18
98
SHOE STORE
Tea & Textiles
Main
Racine
HIGH
SCHOOL

sale
on select
bars &
17109
17
17109

Police work in my community. They keep us safe by enforcing laws and preventing crimes.

Firefighters in my community respond to emergencies and put out fires.

Doctors treat sickness and help people in my community stay well.

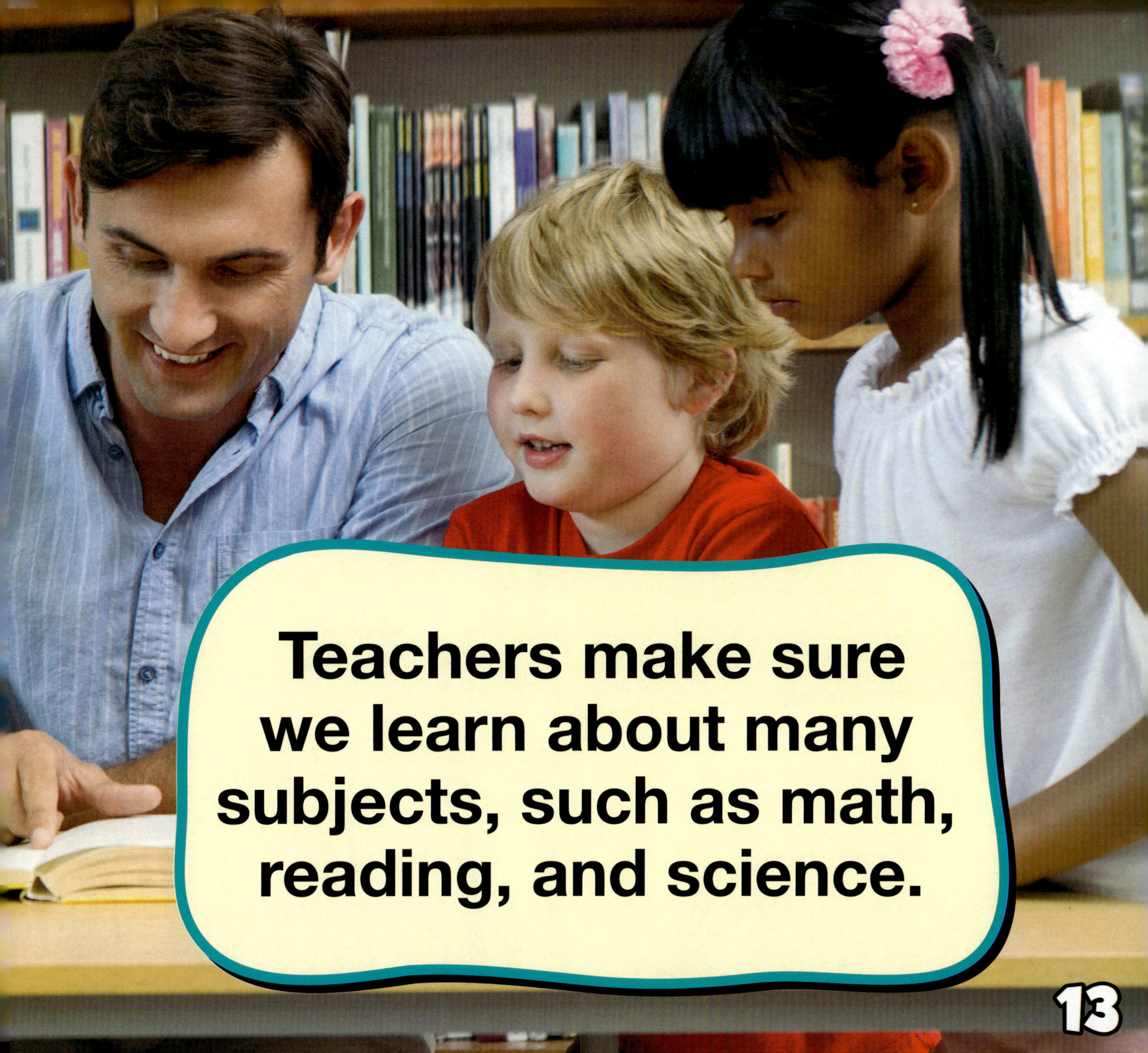

Teachers make sure we learn about many subjects, such as math, reading, and science.

Librarians organize books and help readers choose what to read.

Welcome!
My name is
Susan

Construction workers use tools and machines to build the buildings, bridges, and roads in my community.

doka
Framax
Xlife
GSV
geprüft

Dentists work in my community. Dentists help keep our teeth and gums clean and healthy.

Many people work together to make a community safe and strong.
COMMUNITY DAY

COMMUNITY
DAY
COMMUNITY
DAY

PEOPLE IN MY COMMUNITY BY THE NUMBERS

There are more than **50,000** **fire stations** across the **United States.**

Most **doctors** go to school for about **12 to 14 years** before they start practicing medicine.

The **Library of Congress** has **164 million** titles in its collection.

Fire stations, hospitals, and police stations are open **24 hours** a day.

Many **construction workers** get up as early as **3:30 AM** to start their work.

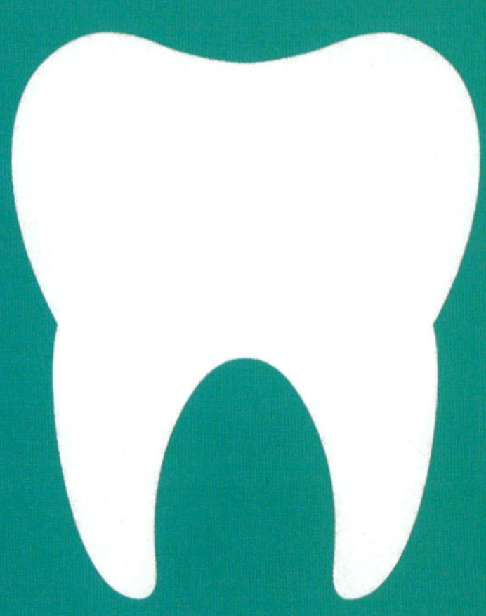

The first dentist lived in ancient **Egypt** in around **2650 BC.**

KEY WORDS

Research has shown that as much as 65 percent of all written material published in English is made up of 300 words. These 300 words cannot be taught using pictures or learned by sounding them out. They must be recognized by sight. This book contains 33 common sight words to help young readers improve their reading fluency and comprehension. This book also teaches young readers several important content words, such as proper nouns. These words are paired with pictures to aid in learning and improve understanding.

Page	Sight Words First Appearance
4	a, and, is, live, people, place, play, where, work
7	by, in, keep, my, they, us
8	out, put, to
11	help, well
12	about, as, learn, make, many, such, we
15	read, what
16	the, use
19	our
20	together

Page	Content Words First Appearance
4	community
7	crimes, laws, police
8	emergencies, firefighters, fires
11	doctors, sickness
12	math, reading, science, subjects, teachers
15	books, librarians
16	bridges, buildings, construction, machines, roads, tools
19	dentists, gums, teeth
20	safe, strong

Watch
Video content brings each page to life.

Browse
Thumbnails make navigation simple.

Read
Follow along with text on the screen.

Listen
Hear each page read aloud.

Go to www.eyediscover.com and enter this book's unique code.

BOOK CODE

AVY84389